SHARKS

HAMMERHEAD SHARKS

JOHN F. PREVOST
ABDO & Daughters

Published by Abdo & Daughters, 4940 Viking Drive, Suite
622, Edina, Minnesota 55435.

Library bound edition distributed by Rockbottom Books,
Pentagon Tower, P.O. Box 36036, Minneapolis, Minnesota
55435.

Printed in the United States.

Cover Photo credit: Peter Arnold, Inc.

Interior Photo credits: Peter Arnold, Inc.

Edited by Bob Italia

Library of Congress Cataloging-in-Publication Data

Prevost, John F.
  Hammerhead sharks / by John F. Prevost. p. cm. — (Sharks)
Includes bibliographical references (p. 23) and index.
  ISBN 1-56239-471-1
1. Hammerhead sharks—Juvenile literature. [1. Hammerhead sharks. 2. Sharks.]
I. Title. II. Series: Prevost, John F. Sharks.
QL638.95.S7P74   1995
597'.31—dc20   95-1171
                                                    CIP
                                                    AC

ABOUT THE AUTHOR

John Prevost is a marine biologist and diver who has been active in conservation and education issues for the past 18 years. Currently he is living inland and remains actively involved in freshwater and marine husbandry, conservation and education projects.

Contents

HAMMERHEAD SHARKS AND FAMILY 4

WHAT THEY LOOK LIKE 6

WHERE THEY LIVE 8

FOOD 10

SENSES 12

BABIES 14

ATTACK AND DEFENSE 16

ATTACKS ON HUMANS 18

HAMMERHEAD SHARK FACTS 20

GLOSSARY 22

BIBLIOGRAPHY 23

INDEX 24

HAMMERHEAD SHARKS AND FAMILY

Sharks are fish without **scales**. A rough covering of **denticles** protects their skin. Sharks do not have any bones. Their skeleton is made of **cartilage**, a tough, stretchy tissue.

Hammerhead sharks are found in warm ocean water. There are 9 different hammerhead shark **species**: winghead shark, scalloped bonnethead, whitefin hammerhead, scalloped hammerhead, scoophead, great hammerhead, bonnethead, smalleye hammerhead, and smooth hammerhead. All of these names describe the strange-looking heads of this shark family.

The hammerhead shark gets its name from its strange-looking head.

WHAT THEY LOOK LIKE

The hammerhead shark's flattened head shape can be rectangular, as in the great hammerhead shark, to shovel-shaped, as in the bonnethead shark. Its 2 round eyes are on the ends of its head.

The 3-foot (92-cm) scalloped bonnethead shark is the smallest hammerhead. The 20-foot (6.1-meter) great hammerhead is the largest. Like most other sharks, the females are larger than the males.

Hammerheads are slim, fast-swimming sharks. They are gray or brown along their backs and sides. Their underbelly is white.

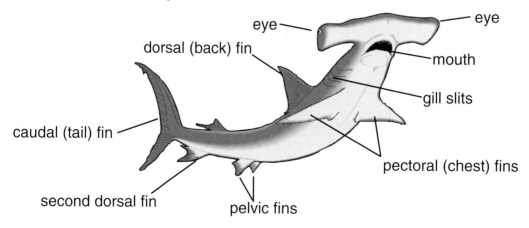

eye — — eye

dorsal (back) fin

mouth

gill slits

caudal (tail) fin

pectoral (chest) fins

second dorsal fin

pelvic fins

The hammerhead shark's flattened head is rectangular or shovel-shaped.

WHERE THEY LIVE

Hammerhead shark **species** are found in **temperate** and **tropical** oceans around the world. They swim in shallow coastal waters to water deeper than 900 feet (275 meters).

Hammerheads are found in **estuaries** and **lagoons**, over **coral reefs**, sandy bottoms and mud flats. They may hunt alone or swim in **schools** of over 100 members.

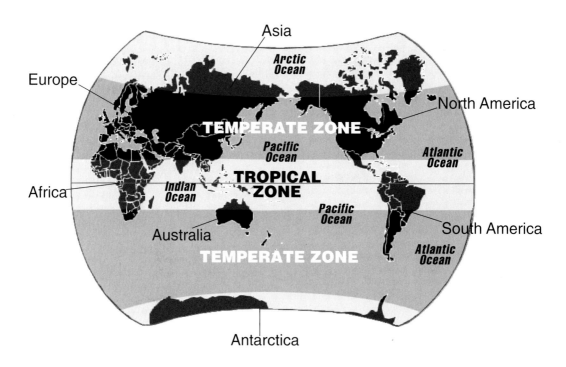

Hammerhead sharks live in shallow, coastal waters and water deeper than 900 feet (275 meters).

Within the cooler areas, hammerhead sharks will **migrate** when water temperatures drop. In the **tropical** areas, some hammerheads will not migrate.

FOOD

All sharks are **predators**. They eat other animals. Hammerhead sharks are skilled hunters. They eat all kinds of **prey** such as catfish, **mullet**, and even **barracuda**. They also eat snails, **squid**, lobsters, and crabs. Some will even feed on other sharks and rays. Hammerheads will also eat dead fish and bait.

Their head shape makes swimming easier. Hammerheads can outswim many other bony fish and sharks. When they hunt in **schools**, even the fastest prey are easily caught.

Some scientists believe that the head shape of the hammerhead helps it to swim better.

SENSES

Hammerhead sharks have great eyesight. The distance between the eyes gives them better **binocular vision**.

Like other sharks, their skin is covered with sense **organs**. The large head surface gives more area for the different sensing cells. These cells sense taste and smell, movement and **electric fields**. Hammerhead sharks can find **prey** in dark or cloudy water with these senses. Even if prey is hidden, a shark can sense the electric field all living animals give off.

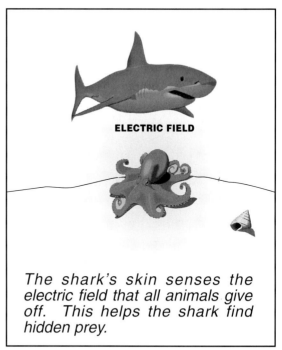

ELECTRIC FIELD

The shark's skin senses the electric field that all animals give off. This helps the shark find hidden prey.

The distance between its eyes gives the hammerhead shark better vision. This helps it find prey in dark or cloudy water.

BABIES

Newborn hammerhead sharks are called pups. The **litter** size is 2 to 37 pups.

Hammerhead pups are born live, not from eggs. They are fed inside their mother through a **yolk sac**.

The females give birth to the pups in shallow water and then swim away. The newborn sharks are 9 to 27 inches (23 to 70 cm) long. Left on their own, the pups will use their well-developed senses to find food and avoid enemies.

An unborn litter removed from a female
hammerhead shark.

ATTACK AND DEFENSE

Hammerheads have blade-like teeth that cut **prey**. The rear teeth of bonnethead sharks can crush shellfish.

Hammerhead sharks have 24 to 37 teeth per row. When a tooth is lost or damaged, a new tooth will replace it. Several rows of new teeth are below the working teeth.

A large whitefin or great hammerhead has almost nothing to fear except man. Smaller hammerheads rely on speed and good senses to avoid larger sharks, bony fish, and sea **mammals**.

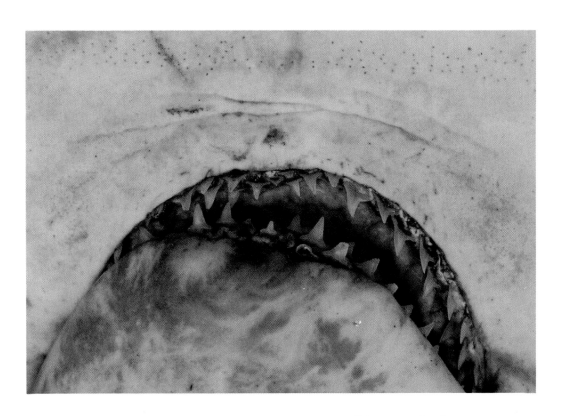

Hammerhead sharks have blade-like teeth that are used to cut their prey.

ATTACKS ON HUMANS

The great, scalloped, and smooth hammerhead sharks are the largest and most dangerous to man. These larger hammerheads do not attack humans unless bait attracts them to an area where people swim.

Hammerhead sharks are easily hooked and netted. Thousands are fished for human food, vitamins, and leather.

The scalloped hammerhead shark is one of the three most dangerous hammerhead shark species.

HAMMERHEAD SHARK FACTS

Scientific Name:

Winghead shark	*Eusphyra blochii*
Scalloped bonnethead	*Sphyrna corona*
Whitefin hammerhead	*S. couardi*
Scalloped hammerhead	*S. lewini*
Scoophead	*S. media*
Great hammerhead	*S. mokarran*
Bonnethead	*S. tiburo*
Smalleye hammerhead	*S. tudes*
Smooth hammerhead	*S. zygaena*

Average Size:

3 to 20 feet (92 cm to 6.1 meters).

Scalloped bonnethead is the smallest at 3 feet (92 cm).

Great hammerhead is the largest and can reach 20 feet (6.1 meters).

Where They're Found: All around the world in **temperate** and **tropical** seas.

A school of hammerhead sharks in the Pacific Ocean near the Galapagos Islands.

GLOSSARY

Barracuda (bair-uh-KOO-dah): A group of long, thin ferocious fish found in warm seas throughout the world.

Binocular (bye-NOK-u-ler) **vision**: Eyesight using two eyes to see distant objects.

Cartilage (CAR-tih-lij): A firm and stretchy tissue, like gristle.

Coral: A hard substance made of skeletons of tiny sea animals, found in tropical waters.

Denticle (DEN-tih-cul): A small toothlike structure that protects a shark's skin and makes it rough to the touch.

Electric field: The electric-charged area surrounding an animal's body, created by the nervous system.

Estuary (ES-tew-air-ee): The mouth of a river where the current meets the sea.

Gill slits: A part of the body of a fish by which it gets oxygen from water.

Lagoon: A shallow body of water partly cut off from the sea by a narrow strip of land.

Litter: Young animals born at one time.

Mammal: A class of animals, including humans, that have hair and feed their young milk.

Migrate: To travel from one region to another in search of food or to reproduce.

Mullet: A group of saltwater and freshwater food fish that have a gray or red torpedo-shaped body.

Organ: A part of an animal or plant that is made up of several kinds of tissue and performs a specific function, like the heart or eyes.

Pelvic fin: A fin found at the lower part of a fish's body.

Predator (PRED-a-tor): An animal that hunts and eats other animals.

Prey: An animal that is hunted for food.

Reef: A narrow ridge of coral at or near the water surface.

Scales: Horny, flattened, platelike structures forming the covering of the fish.

Schools: A large group of fish or water animals of the same kind swimming together.

Species (SPEE-seas): A group of related living things that shares basic characteristics.

Squid: Sea animals related to the octopus that are streamlined in shape and have at least 10 arms.

Temperate (TEM-prit): Moderate to cool water located between the polar and tropical waters.

Tropical (TRAH-pih-kull): The part of the Earth near the equator where the oceans are very warm.

Yolk sac: A pouch containing a food substance for the unborn sharks.

BIBLIOGRAPHY

Budker, Paul. *The Life of Sharks*. London: Weidenfeld and Nicolson, 1971.

Compagno, Leonard. FAO Species Catalogue Vol. 4, *Sharks of the World*. United Nations Development Programme, Rome, 1984.

Gilbert, P. W., ed. *Sharks, Skates, and Rays*. Maryland: Johns Hopkins Press, 1967.

Macquitty, Miranda. *Shark*. New York: Alfred A. Knopf, 1992.

Sattler, Helen. *Sharks, the Super Fish*. New York: Lothrop, Lee & Shepard Books, 1986.

Server, Lee. *Sharks*. New York City Gallery Books, 1990.

Index

B

babies 14
barracuda 10
binocular vision 12
bonnethead shark
    4, 6, 16, 20

C

cartilage 4
catfish 10
color 6
coral reef 8

D

denticles 4

E

eggs 14
electric fields 12
enemies 14
estuaries 8
eyes 6, 12

F

food 10, 18

G

great hammerhead
    4, 6, 16, 18, 20

H

hammerhead shark
    facts 20
head 4, 6, 10, 12
hunter 8, 10

L

lagoons 8
litter 14

M

mammals 16
migrate 9
mullet 10

N

newborn 14

P

predators 10,
prey 10, 12, 16
pups 14

S

scales 4
scalloped bonnethead
    4, 6, 18, 20
schools 8, 10
scoophead shark 4, 20

sense organs 12
size 6, 20
skeleton 4
skin 4, 12
smalleye hammerhead
    4, 20
smooth hammerhead
    4, 18, 20
species 4, 8, 19, 23
squid 10

T

teeth 16
temperate 8, 20
tropical 8, 20

W

whitefin hammerhead 4,
    16, 20
winghead 4, 20

Y

yolk sac 14